The Hippopotamus Book

by Winifred Rosen Casey
pictures by Greg and Tim Hildebrandt

Golden Press • New York
Western Publishing Company, Inc., Racine, Wisconsin

CONTENTS

An African Folktale

In Africa, the Bantu people have a folktale. It is about an unlikely friendship, and it goes something like this:

A hippopotamus, wallowing in the river, feels sad. Nobody could love him, he thinks. He is too fat, too ugly and clumsy.

During the day he floats sadly in the river, protected from the fiery sun. In the moonlight he munches on his grasses, thinking himself the unhappiest of animals, and wishing he were something, anything but a hippopotamus.

He is too busy feeling terrible to notice the egret, never far behind. This slender white bird follows him everywhere. She admires his strength, the beautiful color of his hide and the confident way he moves through the bush. When he returns to the river at dawn, she perches on a branch above his head, and her heart beats quickly with love.

One hot afternoon the hippopotamus has a dream that he is as slender and graceful as a bird. Since it is his favorite, he tries to dream it for as long as he can. Strange noises come from the trees along the bank, but the hippopotamus does not even twitch an ear. Leaves rustle, twigs snap, and suddenly two men appear: hunters with long shining spears.

The hippopotamus, dreaming that he is a bird, sleeps on.

But the egret is awake. She sees the hunters pointing their spears at the sleeping noble hippopotamus. They would kill him for his great ivory-white teeth. Screeching, the egret falls from her branch to slap the water by the hippo's head. He is awakened by her warning. Seeing the men and their gleaming spears he dives deep and gallops away along the bottom of the river.

The hippopotamus swims swiftly downstream to safety, and suddenly his life—which he had never valued before—seems beautiful. He floats to the surface feeling himself as light as a feather in the current, almost as light as the egret herself, just now landing on his nose.

9

Part I: Looking at Hippos

IN ZAIRE

Not long ago, hippopotamuses lived all over Africa. Long ago, they lived in Europe too. Now hippopotamuses live only in the central and eastern half of Africa, in the part below the Sahara Desert.

If you had gone to Africa a couple of hundred years ago, you would have found the great hippopotamus roaming freely over much of the continent. Wherever there was water there were hippopotamuses. Now people live near many of the places where the hippos used to live, and the hippos do not live in these places any longer. In fact, if you were looking for hippopotamuses in Africa today, you would be wise to visit the national parks or game preserves where wild animals are protected by law and no people live. Only in the game preserves would you be likely to find hippopotamuses.

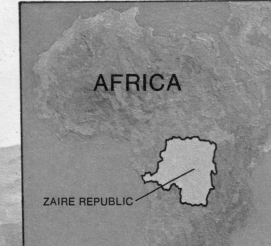

AFRICA

ZAIRE REPUBLIC

But if you did go to a game preserve, the Albert National Park in the Zaire Republic, say, you would find more hippos than you could hope to count using all your fingers and toes, and the fingers and toes of your whole family and all your friends. The Albert National Park has the largest population of hippopotamuses in Africa, and therefore in the world because wild hippopotamuses do not live anywhere in the world except in Africa. That is a fact.

Suppose you decided you just *had* to see these noble beasts in their natural home or habitat. To do so you would have to get on a jet plane and fly to Africa, straight to the Kivu Province of the Zaire Republic.

Because the Zaire Republic is on the equator it would be very hot. The equator is an imaginary circle dividing the earth's surface into two equal halves or hemispheres, a Northern one and a Southern one. All along the equator the seasons vary hardly at all. Even if you arrived in December it would be very hot, and the days and nights would be of equal length because that is the way days and nights are on the equator.

But you would be so happy to have arrived in Africa that you probably wouldn't even object to the heat. In order to see as many hippos as soon as possible, you would get right into a Land Rover (a Jeep) and head for any one of the many lakes, rivers, swamps, bogs, streams, marshes or springs that fill the Albert National Park. You would do a bit of sight-seeing, of course, on your way, passing through rain forests and jungles; under huge, snow-capped volcanoes; through grassy savannas and dry, desert plains. You would see herds of longhorned buffalo on the flatlands; families of olive baboons in the forest trees. The sky would be filled with so many wonderful birds that you would get a crick in your neck from gazing upward all the time.

Nearing the marshy banks of a river, you would want to walk quietly, and pick your way carefully through the wild date palms. If there were hippopotamuses in the river—and there certainly would be if this were a river in a game preserve in Zaire—you would know it

Spectacled Weaver

African Spoonbill

Redbilled Hornbill

Baboons

Marabou Stork

African Buffalo

11

even before you had parted the last line of date palm leaves. You would know it, in fact, a mile away.

Hippopotamuses make a lot of noise

A hippopotamus can open his mouth so wide that you could sit upright on his bottom jaw without even knocking your head against the roof of his mouth. You wouldn't want to make this experiment, of course. It would not be safe. Besides, if the hippopotamus happened to be making one of his loud noises it would hurt your eardrums. Hippos are best at a distance.

So you would want to find yourself a place on the river bank from which to watch the hippopotamuses. Some of them would be underneath the water, with only their eyes and nostrils showing above. They would be asleep. Others would be thrashing around, grunting and bellowing in that deafening way that hippos have. The quiet sleeping ones off to one side would be the females. If you looked closely you would see the little eyes and nostrils of baby hippos asleep on their mothers' backs. The thrashing, noisy hippos would all be males.

Hippopotamuses live in herds and behave the way most animals in herds behave. The females stay more or less quietly apart with their young, and the males fight with each other over the females. This is true of herds of pigs, camels, sheep, goats, deer, cattle, antelope, and giraffes—all of whom are related to hippopotamuses. The reason all these animals are related is that they are all mammals who have an even number of toes on each one of their feet. A giraffe may not, at first glance, look much like a hippopotamus, but they are relatives nevertheless. You can tell by their toes.

Besides having an even number of toes on each of their feet, all of these animals have something else in common which makes them different from all other mammals, and that is the way their teeth are arranged in their mouths. But hippopotamuses' teeth, though they are arranged like those of sheep and giraffes, are larger than the teeth of any other land-dwelling mammal. Their two bottom teeth are so big, so strong, and so white that men used to kill hippos just to get the teeth from their mouths. It is hard to believe that anyone would kill an animal weighing several tons just for a few pounds of ivory teeth, but people did. That is one of the reasons why governments created national parks. In the national parks of the world, visitors are not allowed to kill animals for their teeth, tusks, toes or anything else.

Most of the time hippos use their teeth for eating leaves and grasses, because leaves and grasses are the only kinds of food that wild hippos eat. All animals are classified into one of three groups according to the kind of food they eat. Those like hippos who eat only vegetables are called *herbivores*. Animals who eat only meat, cats for example, are known as *carnivores*, while animals like pigs and people, who eat everything, belong to the class called *omnivores*.

During the mating season, when the male hippopotamuses fight with each other over the female hippopotamuses, they often hurt each other with their teeth. But not as much as you might think. A hippopotamus's skin is nearly two inches thick—almost as thick as your front door.

There is one very special reason why hippos need their extra-long, super-strong teeth.

The reason is crocodiles.

Crocodiles are the largest of all reptiles, and they live in all the places in Africa where hippos like to live. Crocodiles are carnivores.

They eat meat. Now, a big, grown-up hippopotamus needn't worry about being eaten up by a crocodile, because a grown-up hippopotamus is far bigger than a crocodile could ever hope to be. But he was not always so big. When he was born he weighed a mere hundred pounds. That may seem like a lot to you, but to a two-ton crocodile it is the perfect size for a meal.

Luckily, crocodiles rarely make meals out of baby hippos. One reason is that baby hippos spend much of their time resting safely on their mothers' backs. When they are not actually *on* their mothers, they are quite *near* their mothers, and their mothers keep one eye carefully cocked for crocodiles.

You would have been sitting on the river bank for quite a while by now, and still you would not have caught a glimpse of a whole hippo. All you could see of the females are eyes and noses. When the males lift their heads out of the water to bellow you would see their huge necks, tiny ears and, of course, their sparkling teeth. Still, you would be eager to see an entire hippopotamus. I wouldn't blame you, but you would have to wait.

"Wait for what?" you might ask. "Soon it will be dark." And so it will. Dark is just what we *are* waiting for.

Hippopotamuses spend all day in the water for two reasons. The first is that they have very big bodies and rather short legs. Because their bodies are so big they do not like to spend too much time standing up, particularly when it is hot, and particularly when they can float in the water with no effort at all. The other reason is that even though hippopotamuses have skin as thick as your front door, skin thick enough to protect them from crocodiles, the surface of their skin is easily burned by the sun. If a hippo absolutely *must* be out of the water during the day, glands in his skin make a special kind of reddish oil that keeps his hide from drying out. But even with the red oil from his glands he will not be happy in the heat.

15

On a hot day, a hippo is only happy in the water.

At last the sun would go down behind the mountains, and the air would begin to cool. The herd of hippopotamuses would be swimming to the shores now, and you would have to sit very quietly so as not to frighten them. Although it is unlikely that they would see you, for their eyesight is not good, they would be listening carefully as they climbed the bank, and testing the air for strange smells.

If you were lucky, and of course you would be, a hippo would swim to shore just downwind of where you were sitting. Then you would watch him rise slowly out of the river, water gushing down his back, his great barrel-shaped body a glistening gray in the twilight.

At first the sight of a tremendous hippopotamus such a short distance away might be a shock. You would not have been that close to an animal that big before, unless of course it was on the other side of a fence. Now there wouldn't be any fence.

If the hippo were an adult male he would be about fourteen feet long. Now, if a tall man were to stand on the shoulders of another tall man, the two of them together would not be as tall as that hippo is long. In fact, if you stood on the shoulders of the second man, the three of you together would be no taller than the length of the hippopotamus. Which might make you want to say "WOW" or "Look!" or "Get me out of here!!" But you wouldn't. You would sit perfectly still saying nothing at all so as not to disturb the hippo.

Silently you would watch him climb the bank. His great toes would expand so that his feet would not sink too deeply into the mud, and he might grunt a bit now and then because of the effort it takes to move four tons of hippopotamus up a muddy riverbank. Not having eaten all day he would be a very hungry hippo and would climb the bank surprisingly fast. Then he would smell the sweet scent of the panicum grass blowing over the plains, and, turning his great head into the wind, he would trot quickly off, a trail of slender egrets following in his wake.

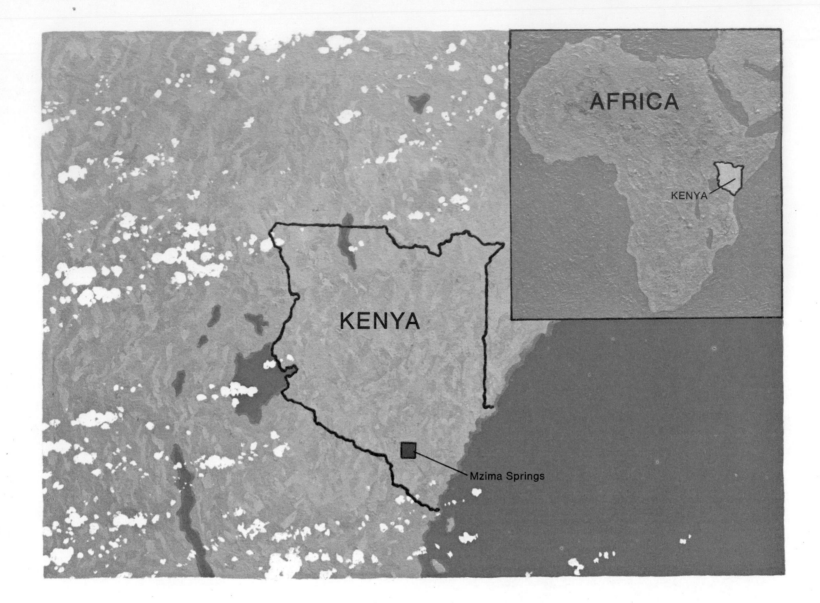

AT MZIMA SPRINGS

Three hundred miles east of the Zaire Republic's eastern border is a country called Kenya which ends at the Indian Ocean. Kenya has fifteen national parks and the largest concentration of animals in Africa. Of all the African parks, Tsavo is the biggest, and it contains the most animals.

The imaginary circle called the equator that divides the earth into two halves (a top and a bottom) passes through Kenya. And so, like Zaire, Kenya is hot all the time, even when it rains, which happens only during two periods of the year.

For a brief time after the spring and winter rains, green grass carpets the equatorial African plains. The trees burst into leaf, and the desert rose blooms. In the Tsavo National Park, a great deal of rain falls on a range of mountains that rises high above the flatlands. These mountains were formed many hundreds of millions of years ago by volcanic eruptions. Now they are big mounds of volcanic ash. Instead of spilling over the sides of the mountains, the rain seeps into the ash like water into a sponge. Deep down in the earth, the water collects into an underground river that flows under the plains for twenty-five miles before gushing out of the earth at a place called Mzima Springs.

Even during the hottest and driest part of the year when Kenya's plains are a sun-scorched, yellowish brown, water rushes out of the ground, forming Mzima's pools and little lakes.

Here, from the vast surrounding plains, the animals come to drink. Some, like the elephant and rhinoceros, march fearlessly into the pools and drink deeply from the cool water. Others, like the zebra or impala, approach the water carefully and drink quickly from the shallow edges. Hidden in the deeper pools the crocodiles lie in wait. They can grab a drinking deer by the leg, or stun it with a blow from their great tails. Nothing, not even a lion, is safe around the sharp-toothed crocodile.

At Mzima's springs, most of the seventy hippos are snoozing quietly. Since the sun is high, they are submerged, raising their nostrils to the surface every forty seconds or so to breathe. Now and then, one of the hippos will blow a great deal of air out of his nose, then sink down and disappear for several minutes, often surfacing again way at the other end of the pool.

Until recently, few could say what hippos looked like or were doing underneath the water all that time. Though everyone was certainly curious, not many people would actually go and look. Most people do not like the idea of swimming with crocodiles and hippopotamuses, not to mention schools of large, gray-green labeo fish, turtles and eels. Some people, though, do not mind.

Two of the people who do not mind are naturalist photographers named Joan and Alan Root. They went to Mzima in 1970 with diving gear and underwater cameras, and they made a film of what they saw for the BBC, which The New York Zoological Society distributes.

Hippopotamuses simply do not make sense until you have seen them (or movies of them) swimming underwater. On the land their huge bodies seem ungainly, even, to some, ridiculous. Not so underwater. Under the water they drift and swim with perfect grace, for it is here that they are most at home.

Hippopotamuses are buoyant. This means that they are able to float on or in the water. The depth at which they float depends upon how much air they have in their lungs. When a hippo wants to sink deeper into the water, he exhales, blowing twin plumes of spray above the surface rather like the single spray of a whale.

Submerged in the lakes at Mzima, the hippos breed, give birth to their young and live out their lives. To move from place to place they use trails they have worn along the lake bottoms, familiar paths they follow with a stately, swaying motion. Like shadows, they glide through the murky pools in utter silence.

Because it is surrounded by miles of waterless plains, Mzima Springs is a fountain of life. When Joan and Alan Root dived beneath the surface, they discovered that the fountain itself was filled with animals, most of whom, like the crocodiles, feed on other animals—smaller animals.

For example: a floating dragonfly catches a tasty gnat, and is then eaten by a fish. The fish is eaten by a bigger fish, who gets eaten by an otter, who is then swallowed by a crocodile. The crocodile is at the very end of something called a food chain. Each animal is a link in that chain. But if the crocodile is the last link, where does the chain begin?

With the hippopotamus, of course.

It is the hippopotamus—the great and gigantic hippopotamus—who is responsible for the lives of the tiniest and most helpless of the creatures. From the land the hippo brings sustenance to the waters. He does it regularly, effortlessly and without anyone telling him to.

Hippopotamuses at Mzima behave in much the same way as you have seen hippopotamuses behaving in Zaire. That is, they stay in the water all day, swimming, sleeping or arguing—depending on their sex and the season of the year. (The males fight with each

other mostly in the fall.) Then, when the sun goes down, the herd lumbers out of the water and heads into the bush lands to find food.

All night long they wander among the baobab trees munching on the sparse grasses. A hippopotamus eats about a hundred and fifty pounds of grass in a single night, if he can get it. That is a lot of grass, several lawns' worth at least. To find that much grass, the herd of hippos fans out over the plains, traveling for as many as ten miles in all directions.

At dawn, they return to the springs and little lakes at Mzima.

Slowly, they lower themselves back into the water, for their bellies are quite full, and they are tired from their all-night journeys.

The blinding sunrise finds them already half asleep, beginning to digest their meals.

Throughout the day, the hippos digest the food they ate the night before. The grass is broken down by enzymes in their stomachs. Then their bloodstreams absorb the proteins, vitamins, and minerals their bodies need. What their bodies do not need or cannot digest is called waste. This waste is expelled into the water.

The nice part of it all is that what the hippos waste is not wasted at all.

Diving and swimming in the pools at Mzima, Joan and Allan Root realized that the rich organic waste covering the bottom provided food for insect larvae (baby gnats, for example) and millions of tiny, fresh water shrimp. Whenever hippos made their way along the bottom, as they often did, they sent thousands of these creatures swirling into the water like clouds. Many tiny creatures may be eaten by one little fish who will be swallowed, perhaps, by a white-tailed kite swooping out of the sky. Beginning with the hippo's generous waste, the food chain joins land to water and all animals to each other: link by living link.

Part II: Getting along with Hippos

It is not easy to photograph hippopotamuses underwater, for hippopotamuses do not like to swim with people any more than most people like to swim with them.

A famous French diver by the name of Jacques Cousteau discovered this when he went to a lake in East Africa called Lake Tanganyika. Lake Tanganyika is the longest freshwater lake in the world, nearly 400 miles long. Hundreds of hippopotamuses live in it. Cousteau thought it would be simple enough to dive into the lake and have a look at the hippos.

He and his crew put on their black rubber wet suits, their masks, fins, and aqua lungs so that they would be able to stay underwater long enough to film the hippos' habits. But as soon as the men dived into the water, the hippos swam away, stirring up (as is their habit) the bottom of the lake, and making the water so muddy the men couldn't even see them, much less take their pictures.

The men who had come all the way from Europe to East Africa just to film hippos were distressed. But they didn't despair. Instead, they thought up a daring new plan in order to sneak up on the herd unnoticed.

From Paris, Captain Cousteau ordered a life-size plastic model of a hippopotamus to be flown to him at Lake Tanganyika. The plastic hippo was hollow and roomy enough for two men to get inside of it. Because it had been constructed with no bottom jaw, the man in front could look through his camera and shoot movies of other (real) hippopotamuses from the false hippopotamus's mouth.

It didn't work though.

As soon as the herd of hippos saw the plastic dummy coming toward them they dived and swam away as fast as they could, leaving the photographers with more muddiness and clouds and disappointment.

Lake Tanganyika, the men decided, was the problem. It was too big for filming hippos. They would have to go inland to a small river where the hippos could not escape from them and their cameras so easily.

But even in the small inland river the divers had a difficult time. For one thing, the men were afraid of the hippos. For another, the hippos were afraid of the men. And everyone was afraid of the crocodiles.

Another plan was called for, and so the men built a raft. To the bottom of the raft they attached an underwater camera. Then with ropes from the shore, they guided the raft toward a group of hippos.

It didn't work though.

When the hippos saw the raft closing in on them they got frightened and moved away. As it came closer they were forced to the very bank of the river, and this they did not like at all.

Animals do not like being backed into corners.

It upsets them.

Any animal forced far enough into a corner will, sooner or later, turn around and fight.

Hippos are no exception to this rule.

Eventually, the group of hippos refused to be pushed any farther. It would take something very powerful to force a herd of hippos out of their water in the middle of a hot East African day. It would take something a great deal more powerful than a floating raft to do that. And so the hippos stopped and stood their ground in the shallow water. Then they charged . . .

The raft of course did not survive. The camera, too, was broken, and most of the underwater film was ruined. In his movie, "Hippo!" Captain Cousteau tells us in the beginning about how dangerous hippos are. Then we see pictures of angry hippopotamuses charging and destroying his equipment. It is all very terrible and exciting.

But the interesting part of it all is that Joan and Alan Root, who had quite a different attitude about hippos, managed to take a great many pictures of hippopotamuses going about their perfectly ordinary business underwater at Mzima. Joan Root even took pictures of Alan Root petting a sleeping male hippopotamus's back.

The Roots were very patient and calm. They lived at Mzima for several weeks, studying the habits and the behavior of all the animals. And they did not fail to observe the one and only cardinal rule concerning hippos.

The cardinal rule concerning hippos is this:
NEVER GET BETWEEN A HIPPO AND THE WATER.

This is important to remember if you are thinking of encountering any hippopotamuses in the course of your travels. Hippopotamuses, after all, are the second largest of the three biggest land-dwelling animals.

The first largest is the elephant.

The third largest is the rhinoceros.

You might imagine that animals with horns as strong as rhinos', tusks as long as elephants', and teeth as sharp as hippos', would always feel calm and secure. You would be mistaken.

The fact is that all of them are easily frightened, and all of them are dangerous when they are afraid.

Hippos are not so dangerous as elephants and rhinos. Hippos are not frightened by as many things as elephants and rhinos. What hippos are frightened of, though, is things that get between them and their water. Hippos are very attached to their water, as we have already noticed. Without their water to float around in, their legs get tired and their skins get burned by the sun.

So, if a herd of hippos happens to be lolling about in the mud along the shore, and a boat happens to come between them and the deep part of their river or pool, they will see that boat as a threat to their very survival.

For the hippo, water equals life and something that comes between him and his life threatens him with death. Threatened with death, the hippo attacks.

So, when Captain Cousteau floated his raft toward the group of hippos, forcing them to the shore and getting between them and their water, he was threatening their survival and they behaved accordingly.

Luckily, the Roots never put themselves between the hippos and their deep pools at Mzima Springs. Approaching from the shore, the Roots got to see hippopotamuses swaying gracefully along underwater trails, their great legs paddling through the water in a gait like a horse's trot, their giant toes silently scraping the bottom so as to stir up food for the hungry fish.

And the crocodiles barely bothered the picturetakers at all.

31

Part III: Understanding Hippos

THE GODDESS TAURET

Many, many centuries ago, when hippopotamuses lived in more places than they do now, the Egyptians worshiped a goddess who looked like a female hippopotamus. She was named Tauret, and she was the goddess of childbirth and motherhood. Sometimes Tauret was pictured standing on her hind legs holding a roll of papyrus, a symbol of protecting. Her image was especially popular in Thebes, on the Nile, the ancient capital of Upper Egypt.

Sometimes, though, the motherly, protective Tauret was drawn by the Egyptians as an angry or "avenging" goddess, one who punished the Egyptians' enemies. Then they gave Tauret the body of a hippopotamus and the head of a lioness. And just in case a hippopotamus with a lioness's head wasn't sufficiently terrifying, Tauret brandished a dagger in the air.

The Egyptians understood hippopotamuses.

Whether they are in Zaire, in Mzima, Tanganyika, or the Nile, hippopotomuses are considerate enough to provide the main source of food for the tiny creatures that nourish the fish that nourish the larger animals. Because they eat only vegetables, hippos link the long, complicated food chains to the dry earth.

And so the hippopotamus is a perfect symbol for motherhood and fertility.

But a mother doesn't only create life; she must also defend it. And hippopotamus mothers are perfect examples of this rule.

Like Tauret with her dagger, the mother hippo will charge even the most terrible of crocodiles if that crocodile happens to look hungrily at her calf.

BIRTH AND GROWTH

The mature female hippopotamus gives birth to one very small calf each year. The calf is born, as it was conceived, in the water. It is born after a gestation period of 233 days (about 8½ months). The gestation period is the amount of time it takes the embryo of an animal to develop inside its mother's body.

The hippopotamus has a shorter gestation period than human beings, whose embryos take nine months to develop. Hippos have a very short gestation period considering how very large they are. It takes an elephant, for example, nearly two years to get ready to be born.

But elephants are not born in the water. As soon as an elephant is born it must be able to follow the movements of the herd across the plains or through the African bush. A baby elephant cannot float about nursing all day, or climb upon its mother's back for protection.

The single calf of the hippopotamus weighs only a small fraction (about 1/70th) of what it will weigh when it is grown up. It weighs about 100 pounds at birth, about 7,000 by the time it is mature, four or five years later. When it is born it is very helpless, almost as helpless as human beings are when they are born.

But hippopotamuses learn to take care of themselves much more quickly than do human beings, though not so quickly as elephants. Within a few days a hippo learns to swim in the water, wallow in the mud, and walk well enough on land to follow its mother when she goes to graze in the moonlight.

For the first year, the small calf is protected from dangers by its mother. For during the day the crocodiles float—still as logs and nearly as fearless—while at night the lions roam.

By the time the calf is two months old it is living on grass like its mother, rather than on her milk, and it is gaining about 10 pounds every day. By the end of a year, the young hippo is big enough to take care of itself.

Now, as you so carefully (and quietly) observed from your spot on the river bank in Zaire, hippo herds are divided according to sex. When male calves get to be a year old they leave the herd of females and go off to swim, wallow, and graze alone. The females all stay together in a big group.

Suppose you went back to Zaire, and (after carefully picking your way through the familiar date palm leaves) you found your spot upon the river bank. If you had lots of time and enough patience to sit still day after day, you would begin to notice that the male part of the hippo herd has its own special kind of order. It is called a social hierarchy. The strongest and fiercest males are at the top of the arrangement. The way they get to the top is by winning fights with other (weaker) males.

The strongest and fiercest males, the ones at the top of the social order, have the right to swim and float quite close to the females. Each one learns just how close he can get, and gets as close as he can.

The younger and weaker the male, the lower he is on the hierarchy, and the more distance he must keep between himself and

Great White Pelican

the center of the herd of females. Now and then, in imitation of their elders, the young males will thrash about in mock combat.

Watching from the bank day after day, week after week, you would often see the older hippos threatening each other with gaping mouths and loud, bellowing cries. Sometimes one hippo would prove himself superior simply by gaping wider and bellowing louder than his opponent. If this didn't work, he would fight seriously for his status in the ranks of the herd.

By the time a male is four years old he has reached his full size, twelve to fourteen feet long, four to five feet tall. He is now sexually mature, an adult ready to rise through the ranks and court the favors of the females.

Mature females are capable of bearing a calf every year for twenty years or more. Each calf is conceived in the fall and born the following spring. Throughout the spring and early summer, the mother nurses her calf, protects it, and tells it all the lessons hippos have to hear.

By the following fall the calf is five times his original size, and on its own. Whether or not the mother will then mate with the same bull who fathered her last calf will depend upon his place in the order of the herd. If the bull has grown stronger and fiercer he might prefer a younger cow to his previous mate. Or, perhaps he was an old bull whose strength might have begun to fail, in which case a younger hippo might have taken over his territory.

But whether she mates with a young hippo of twelve, eager and in his prime, or with a wise and battle-scarred veteran of thirty-five, the cow will conceive another calf.

THE HIPPO AND THE HERD

Watching from your river bank day after day, week after week and year after year, you would observe that only the strongest and fiercest hippos are able to mate and breed. This pattern was first described by the scientist Darwin as being part of the Process of Natural Selection.

It takes great strength and courage to be a successful hippopotamus. The qualities of strength and courage are therefore *selected* by a natural process: that of the strong and fierce males driving off the weak, sickly, or frightened ones.

Nature uses many means of selecting the animals best fitted for survival. Carnivores like lions, for example, prey mainly on the very young or old, the lame and sick, or the unwary members of a species. By such means the hippos' numbers are kept in check, and a balance is insured between the herd and its environment.

The size of any given herd is the result of the balance of many things: such as how large a body of water the hippos inhabit, how much vegetation the surrounding land supports, and how many other animals are competing for the same food supply.

Everything contributes to the balance: the minerals in the earth, the amount of rain, the number of crocodiles.

Now, when the balance is upset, as it must be from time to time, everything is thrown out of whack for a while.

For example, the number of animals in an area might suddenly increase due to a distant brush fire. Such an increase would temporarily shake the balance between the land and the animals feeding off it. Such upsets occur frequently in Africa, often causing violent shifts in the delicate relationship of all the living things.

A sudden migration of game into an area with a limited food supply will make it difficult for all the animals to get enough to eat. If the hippos are eating less, they will deposit less organic waste in the water. Fewer insects will be born, the number of fish will decrease, and the hungry crocodiles will go to greater lengths to catch baby hippos.

But even violent disruptions of delicate balances are adjusted in time. Gradually the weaker members of the various species will die off, and there will be more food to go around. The hippos will find more grass, deposit richer waste, encourage more insects to be born with which to feed more fish and satisfy the hunger of the crocodiles.

If the river is large and the land fertile enough, hippo herds can grow huge in number. Hippos reproduce quickly and live for as many as fifty years.

From the banks of some rivers in Zaire, or the edges of certain brackish swamps in the East African country of Uganda, you would be amazed to see dense herds of hippopotamuses.

Though many of their great, balloonlike bodies would be invisible from above, you would notice birds, like little flags, indicating the presence of hundreds of hippos just beneath the surface of the water.

Gleaming white in the bright sunshine, the egrets (and often, too, the much smaller oxpeckers) walk back and forth, pecking daintily at insects, even sipping water from the little pools that have formed upon the sleeping hippos' backs.

Below the surface, schools of labeo fish vacuum a layer of green algae off the hippos' hides.

But inside the huge, buoyant cushions of their bodies, the hippos seem unaware of the attention they are getting.

Just before they dive, they send up their plumes of airy spray. Then the birds take flight with a cry as their floating islands disappear into the deeps.

Part IV: Appreciating Hippos

HIPPOS, HORSES AND PYGMY HIPPOS

Hippopotamus is Greek for "riverhorse": the *hippo* part means horse, and *potamus* is the Greek word for river.

It is an odd name, for hippos and horses are not near-relatives. Horses have only one toe and an entirely different arrangement of teeth from that of hippos. Horses have hair all over their bodies while hippos have only a few tufts of bristles on their noses and chins. Though horses can swim, their life cycles take place entirely on land, whereas all of the important events in a hippo's life occur in water.

Horses come in many different breeds and vary greatly in size, color and temperament. There are small, spotted Appaloosas, for example; massive chestnut-brown Clydesdales, strawberry roans, and snow-white Arabians. Some horses have thick coats to protect them from the mountain cold, while others have been bred to endure the fiercest desert heat.

But there are only two kinds of hippopotamuses: very big hippopotamuses and very small hippopotamuses.

The very small ones, which are called pygmy hippopotamuses, weigh only ten pounds at birth and get about as big as a large pig by the time they are mature three years later. Being only thirty inches tall and four to five feet in length, pygmy hippopotamuses look like miniatures of their gigantic relatives. They are so appealing and attractive looking in fact, that any hippopotamus-lover who stumbled upon a pygmy hippo would undoubtedly want to take it home and keep it as a pet.

Arabian

Clydesdale

Appaloosa

This would be a mistake. Pygmy hippos are very solitary creatures who do not display any affection for other animals. They stay hidden deep in the deepest forests of Liberia, the same forests in fact that are inhabited by a dwarfish tribe of people who are also called pygmies because they are so much smaller than most other people.

No one can really explain why these species are so small (adult pygmy people are generally less than five feet tall) but one theory is that due to the dense vegetation, very little air, water and sunlight reach the forest inhabitants, and this has prevented them from reaching normal size.

The chances are that you wouldn't stumble upon a pygmy hippo even if you traveled all the way to Liberia, and even if you took a machete and hacked your way through the thick vegetation hoping to find one. Unlike their huge relatives, pygmy hippos do not live in herds, but stay silently by themselves or with a single mate, spending a good part of the day in the dark forest pools or in secluded, swampy hideouts. Like the big hippos, though, the pygmies emerge at night to forage for their food.

Except for his extremely small size and rather anti-social nature, the pygmy hippo is just like a regular hippo, which is to say, hardly like a horse at all.

Besides the differences in appearance, there is something else which makes both kinds of hippos unlike any kinds of horses, and that is their relationships with people.

Horses almost always have relationships with people. Hippos almost never do.

Have you ever seen a hippo saddled and bridled?

Do hippos pull plows?

Haul hay?

Herd cows?

Naturally not!

People can, of course, frighten hippos into running away, and people can put up iron fences to make hippos stay in one place. But a hundred-and-sixty-pound man cannot subdue the will of a seven-thousand-pound hippopotamus. That is a fact.

And yet, when the Greeks looked at hippos they were reminded of horses and gave them the name "river horses," and the Greeks were very clever at observing things. What reminded them of horses was not the hippos' hairless hides, their toes, teeth or their tails. For none of these things are in the least horselike, as we have seen. What *is* horselike about a hippo is the nobility of his bearing and the extreme sensitivity of his nature. In these, and in his graceful and bouyant movements underwater, the hippo is wonderfully like a horse indeed.

FOSSILS FROM THE PAST

In prehistoric times, during what geologists call the Pliocene Period, which is part of what is known as the Tertiary Era, hippos roamed throughout the Old World of Europe, even as far north as London. During this period dramatic changes were occurring in the geology of the earth. Some of our most spectacular mountain ranges such as the Alps of Europe and the Himalayas in Asia were being formed, and the fossils (bones or footprints preserved in the earth's crust) dating from this time suggest that in East Africa the sheep were as big as cows, the pigs as large as rhinos and there were hippos twice the size that hippos are today—much larger than the largest living elephant.

Whales, which are the biggest mammals in the world, may be descendants of giant prehistoric hippopotamuses who found their way to the sea and liked it so much they stayed there. Some kinds of whales have four small bones in their flippers which (who knows?) might once have been the toes of a hippopotamus.

HIPPOS OF TODAY

Today the hippo's territory, like the hippo himself, has shrunk. African hippos are in competition for a relatively small supply of fresh water with an ever-increasing population of people. Fortunately, people are beginning to realize that a few neighborly hippos can be a great advantage. Hippos create excellent trails through the jungle and keep the lakes they inhabit free of choking weeds and filled with tasty fish. Though we know that hippos can eat as many as a hundred pounds of grass and assorted plants in a single night, they do not—unlike many other animals—destroy the vegetation by pulling up its roots.

As for the crops of the African farmers, these could be easily protected by small fences, because it is well known that hippos will not and cannot jump over a fence, and that they would not and definitely could not burrow underneath one.

The fact that hippos are so very big leads some people to imagine that they are dangerous, while some other people think of them as comical.

But no matter what these people might happen to think, you know that hippos have a definite place in the pattern of life in the world.